MCKINSEY 7S FRAMEWORK

Boost business performance, prepare for change and implement effective strategies

Written by Anastasia Samygin-Cherkaoui
In collaboration with Anne-Christine Cadiat
Translated by Carly Probert

Business **50MINUTES**.com

MCKINSEY 7S FRAMEWORK   1

Key information
Introduction

THEORY   3

Strategy
Structure
Systems
Staff
Style
Skills
Shared values
Conclusion

LIMITATIONS AND EXTENSIONS   13

Limitations and criticisms
Related models

PRACTICAL APPLICATION   15

Advice and top tips
Case study

SUMMARY   23

FURTHER READING   25

MCKINSEY 7S FRAMEWORK

KEY INFORMATION

- **Names:** 7S, 7-S Framework, the McKinsey 7S Framework.
- **Uses:** management of medium and large organisations, adaptation to change.
- **Why is it successful?** It is easy to represent visually and very applicable.
- **Key words:** organisation, model, management, change.

INTRODUCTION

History

The McKinsey 7S framework dates back to the 1980s, and was first introduced in an article co-authored by Robert Waterman, Thomas Peters and Julien Philips, *Structure is not Organization* (1980). It appeared at a time when the strategy and organisation of a company were the main focus. In fact, it involves rethinking the whole organisation of a business, not simply rearranging the practices in use.

Today, these graphs and diagrams – flowcharts, process, etc. – are widespread in the economic environment, but at the time, it was a stroke of genius for two reasons:

- firstly, the representation of the model in the form of an atom was surprisingly original;
- secondly, the repetition of the same initial letter 'S' for each of the elements creates an alliteration effect.

Both of these features make it easier to memorise the concept and visualise the structure of its seven elements. Ultimately, they contribute to its fame and longevity.

Definition of the concept

The McKinsey 7S framework, developed by the consultancy firm McKinsey, is an organisational diagnosis tool, shown schematically in the form of an atom. The name of the concept highlights, using a simple mnemonic device, both the number of framework elements and its constituents, which all begin with the letter 's'.

GOOD TO KNOW

Founded in 1926, McKinsey is a strategy consultancy firm presented as being at a high-level as it is intended primarily for internationally active companies, at the head of which it is not rare to find former McKinsey employees.

THEORY

An important part of the success of the McKinsey 7S Framework lies in the depiction of the model in the shape of an atom: this image is dynamic and shows the simple and almost obvious interconnection between the elements that make it up. Without dismissing them, it dramatically distances itself from diagrams in the shape of a chain, which show the division of tasks and speed-based productivity gains, and from traditional pyramid flow charts, even if these now increasingly incorporate information flows.

Since the 1930s, studies have highlighted the importance of human relationships. They lead to the inevitable conclusion that it is a mistake to believe in simply professional connections. In fact, relationships and interests that go beyond the theoretical framework of the organisational structure develop between workers or groups of workers. These relationships can certainly be friendly, but also often influential. In other words, they depend on the ability of a person to change the behaviour of another, knowingly or not, to promote their objectives or values. Unpredictable for managers, these relationships are extremely important as they are able to change the organisation as a whole. Each of us can attest to this by recalling situations where individuals within a group changed their behaviour, which then modified everyone's results. Take the example of sport, where changing coach can lead to different results, although the team remains the same and each member retains their function.

Similarly, companies change and, therefore, their needs change. Of course, the basics remain the same: there are still family businesses, companies with highly standardised tasks, companies based on competencies (where the capital gain is made, for example, with intellectual services) and results-orientated companies. The change that occurs is the result of a combination of pre-existing models and appears through increasingly hybrid structures. In addition, most of the time, internationalisation and globalisation are on the rise. A supermarket, for example, operates with some autonomy (each element of the structure is a structure in itself), but is part of a much larger organisation (a national group in our example) that contains it, and is sometimes also included in an even larger structure (international level).

It is in this context that the 7S model appears:

The components of the model

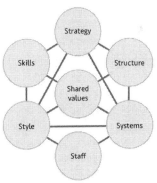

In practice, this representation emphasises the interaction between the different components, each linked to the others, but with a central core. This core deserves some attention for one moment. Originally, the inner circle represented 'extraordinary objectives'. Tony Athos (1934-2002), a professor at Harvard Business School and close friend of Robert Waterman (co-founder of the model), had the idea to change these objectives to 'shared values'. This contribution was not insignificant: it changed the philosophy of the model by replacing prospective elements (objectives) with solid foundations (values).

The seven terms were the result of extensive reflection and debate, and were obviously not chosen at random.

STRATEGY

Strategy determines the means to be deployed. In this case, defining it has to come before all other elements. It is a form of a company's response to its environment: should it reduce costs, produce in large quantities or target its audience? Expand its business or specialise? Is it aggressive towards competitors or does it attempt to differentiate itself?

We can see that the strategy is both crucial and potentially challenging, as it is a result of the interaction between the company and its environment. However, there is no need to be hasty, as strategy guides choices, particularly in terms of investments, product positioning or geographical location. Therefore, it cannot suddenly change.

There are three types of strategy:

- cost leadership
- differentiation (value)
- focus (niche).

A poorly or badly defined strategy can lead to difficult choices, unjustifiable investments, certain skills being emphasised at the expense of others, etc. This may cause a certain lack of unity: the company then has no specialisation or particular point of differentiation. Conversely, a clear strategy leads to investments and decisions that are heading in a specific direction. If the strategy is relevant, the mission has been successful. Otherwise, it is likely that the company will struggle to reform.

To illustrate this, we will return to the example of supermarkets: some brands are distinguished by their low prices, while others are known for the quality and originality of their products. Others do not have any particularly distinctive features. The same reasoning can be applied to computers or phones: some brands are trying to differentiate themselves, either through their style or through their own unique technical specifications. Thus, they specialise and cater to a certain type of user. Others are in competition with various actors who are well established in the market and have to stand out by playing on factors (possibly combined) such as price or accessories – applications or other material or immaterial extras, which give the impression of belonging to a community of users (hence the development of roles such as community manager). However, we can believe that, even if they are intended for a potentially larger audience, they retain fewer customers.

STRUCTURE

When developments and changes are made to business models, the very definition of the structure is changed. Furthermore, employees should be educated so that they perceive the overall strategy of the company and decide for themselves how they will fit into the structure, i.e. how and with whom they will work.

Currently, decentralisation is becoming increasingly widespread in the industry sector. Divisions by function and by product have actually been replaced by other possible segmentations using criteria such as countries, regions, markets, populations, product types, etc. Moreover, the divisions are not necessary mutually exclusive (to take the example of supermarkets: a brand can set up a geographical division with subdivisions according to product within each entity).

Given this situation, it is all the more important for the company to centralise its choices, although generally the strategy will be unique to each division. This enables it to act globally, leaving it up to entities of other levels to develop in their own territory. We can call this a temporary structure, showing relative flexibility, as it is more political or contingent, i.e. it adapts to its environment.

GOOD TO KNOW

- According to structuralism, social relations are organised in social constructions, without the people involved even realising. In humanities, the concept of structure appeared in France in the 1950s. It involves, for the structuralist thinkers – namely Émile Benveniste (1902-1976), Clause Lévi-Strauss (1908-2009), Roland Barthes (1915-1980) and Laurice Godelier (born in 1934) – a highlight of the organisation in which the relationship predominates.

- In biology, one of the peculiarities of the structure is that it regulates itself.

Similarly, the structure adapts to the events it encounters. The relationship aspect is predominant. While the notion of a 'system' predicted the pre-existing elements between which different relationships were established, structuralism somehow goes a step further: here the social constructions are the result of a set of abstract rules and the origin of the structure merges with its operation, so that any disturbance causes spontaneous adaptation.

SYSTEMS

This concept refers to the procedures and operations that make up the daily life of a business. In a sense it involves following or tracking: budget systems, monitoring compliance with internal procedures, legal watch, etc. A strategy that does not account for these procedures is doomed to failure, regardless of its relevance, since it ignores the actual operation of the business. Also, if you decide to change the operation of a business or to simply analyse it, do not neglect the procedures and the follow-up of certain aspects.

STAFF

The concept of staff refers to the team, in the broad sense: it actually encompasses the skills, knowledge, training programmes, motivation, behaviour, wages, hierarchy, evaluation and promotion of individuals. In reality, it refers to human resources management as a whole.

STYLE

This feature, similar to that of staff, relies on a distinction of levels, since it means highlighting the behaviour of top managers. This differentiation between managers and staff can be regrettable, as it separates them, although it is necessary to recognise the potential impact of changing leader on a group. Some will object that the importance of style does not only come from leaders. There are several examples that show this: in a sports team, one player may have a stronger personality or a clearer style than the coach. Similarly with cinema, a secondary role may have more of an impact than a starring role. But does a director not use his expertise to let these characters express themselves? And what about power plays in the world of politics?

GOOD TO KNOW: TOP MANAGEMENT AND TOP MANAGERS

Top management refers to the highest level of the executive functions of a private or public company. Top managers are often strong personalities, capable of uniting their teams and sharing their vision for the future and the means to achieve these objectives. If they make decisions about the strategy and business objectives, they must also (theoretically) take responsibility for them: they are the only person responsible for the success or failure of their policies.

SKILLS

The term 'skills' can also refer to knowledge because it encompasses know-how and interpersonal skills. Again, the concept is similar to those of staff and strategy, but not entirely.

Skills include:

- specifics of the company or brand (the elements which differentiate or are intended to differentiate the company from its competitors);
- staff skills: the company is looking for employees with attitudes and skills which might convey and reinforce its values.

Therefore, this concept involves highlighting the links between the qualities of the people involved and those of the structure in which they operate and to whose development they contribute.

SHARED VALUES

Shared values are at the core of the model. One of the criticisms made against structuralism points out the negligence towards employees, who are considered in some way simply as contingencies of the structure. In response to this, several sociologists, led by Pierre Bourdieu (1930-2002), set out to revalue employees, not to the extent that they can be free of the structures, but considering the scope of their experience and performance as an integral part of the reality of the structure.

Certainly, not everyone is lucky enough to have the job or situation of their choice. However, there must be a minimum of shared values, whether that be the quality of the service or product, or even the company's commitment to a particular cause. Imagine working in a shop where, on Tuesday, you undo all the work you did on Monday. As long as you ignore the futility of your work, there is a good chance you will be able to go on, with varying motivation, possibly even with goals in terms of productivity or quality. On the other hand, what if you became aware of the utter absurdity of what is required of you? Would you continue? For how long? Under what conditions? Similarly, we have mentioned strategy and management: a change at this level can generate staff dissatisfaction (strikes, increased absenteeism, lower productivity, decreased quality of work, departure of workers who have that option, etc.). Everyone who reads this will be able to think of examples, in the present or the past, which illustrate how values that are no longer commonly shared cause tensions or divides.

What matters most here is the link between the values of a company (conveyed by a set of individuals) and the values of companies (or businesses) as commercial or membership organisations. We could refer to companies (with a lower case 'c') and Companies (with an upper case 'C'), the values of the first effectively being a variation of the values of the second, in relation to which they must make sense.

CONCLUSION

Since all the components of the model are interconnected, changing one of them has a direct impact on all the others. This framework must, therefore, always be considered dynamic. Its illustration, in the form of an atom, allows the user to apply the model starting with any element, depending on the information available and the user's position, even if the central component of shared values is significant.

In conclusion, after an analysis of the McKinsey 7S framework, it is possible to get an overall idea of the basis of a company or organisation.

LIMITATIONS AND EXTENSIONS

LIMITATIONS AND CRITICISMS

According to the founding article of the McKinsey 7S framework, *Structure is not Organization* (1980), referring to the Belgian surrealist painter René Magritte (1898-1967), the representation of something is not the thing itself. By extension, this schematic representation of an organisation, as practical and well thought out as it is, is not actually the organisation. Thus, the McKinsey 7S framework is no different from any other, the philosopher's stone of business success. However, as it integrates subjective information (included in the shared values, team, skills, etc.), we believe that this model may adapt better than others to the specific case of each company, since it is able to integrate the specific parameter of 'company culture'. The top management, subject to attention with its own component (style), may be overrepresented because, to some extent, it could also be included in 'staff'.

Following the actionist design, which highlights the importance of human relationships, the organisational theory, in which the 7S framework resides, is only one part of action theory, as developed by sociologists such as Max Webster (1864-1920) in Germany, Talcott Parsons (1902-1979) in the US or Michael Crozier (1922-2013) and Erhard Friedberg (born in 1942) in France.

RELATED MODELS

Given the success of schematic frameworks, some are re-claiming existing models to adapt to their own businesses. In manager presentations, frameworks like 7S are regularly seen. In management, flowcharts – diagrams showing activity as a whole – and process sheets reveal similar reasoning.

Also, more and more models intend to also play on sound, by using alliteration or questions (who, when, how, how much) in order to be memorable.

In our view, what matters in the McKinsey 7S framework is accurately presenting the interconnections between the different concepts, as well as considering the importance of human relationships – it does not prevent, in practice, everyone from doing so in their own way. Referring to a tried and tested model does not mean uniformly applying it.

PRACTICAL APPLICATION

ADVICE AND TOP TIPS

In concrete terms, what does it mean when you decide to create or reform the 7S of a company in the context of a project?

Where to start?

Case 1: Starting a business

If I created a company tomorrow, I would probably take an intellectual approach. In a 'meta' position, where I am both an actor and an external observer, I would define my strategy by first asking the following questions:

- What is my product?
- What is my position in relation to my (potential) competitors?

Theoretically, questions about values would then probably come to mind, followed by the other components of the model. However, in practice, it is clear that we do not always have the opportunity to proceed in this way.

Case 2: An existing business

In an existing structure, it seems more relevant to start from the core of the atom, meaning values. In fact, these are effectively the lowest common denominator of the company's members. Thus, a reflection on the shared values will, first of all, obviously clarify what is shared by the employees. Naturally, answering the question of values and deciding to partially modify their content can influence the strategy, as well as everything else. For example: should we keep a service that is not profitable? Spontaneously, we may be tempted to answer in the negative. But in the case of a medical service or a transport service, this question takes on another meaning.

Implementing the project

As for the creation of a project for a change in an existing structure, dialogue with employees is a prerequisite. Acting in reverse, a sort of 'top down' approach, amounts to wanting to do good for people in spite of themselves. Totalitarian regimes have shown over and over again that this system does not work. Even if the desired change is relevant, the method used to achieve it can doom it to fail.

Now that we know the business a bit better, we must ask the right questions to implement our project:

- What are the different steps involved?
- What are the financial means and resources (staff and skills) needed to achieve this?
- What is special about the structure?

- What differentiates it from its competitors?
- How does it affect those who interact with it?

By answering these questions, we are defining or redefining the style of the company which is directly related to its values. The strategy, in turn, cannot be determined without consideration of values, skills and the environment (competition) in which it will develop.

Evaluating the project

To evaluate the project, it is vital to analyse the system (monitoring and procedures) in order to acquire a comprehensive overview of the whole company, with its qualities and flaws.

Reflection on the 7S criteria inevitably leads to the maintenance or modification of the structure which provides a framework for the action.

The questions raised and the responses given illustrate the interconnections of different concepts in the McKinsey 7S framework. If, in the end, we find that all the elements were considered, specifying exactly what falls within one element or another can sometimes seem complicated. What matters most is remembering not to neglect any aspect of the model.

CASE STUDY

We will now look at company X, an actor in the public sector and therefore a public company. Various external reports point to major management problems, the main indicators of this being:

- a reduction in liquid assets;
- deficient human resources management, in the sense that the number of workers has increased continually over several years for an unchanged service;
- payroll equal to 50% of turnover.

X, a public company, is subject to some control and must be accountable for the issues in its management that raise questions. This creates tensions between the company and its administrative supervision. At the same time, internally, the company is experiencing a change of the Chairman of the Board of Directors (BOD).

Seeking to reassure the administrative supervision, and perhaps also break free from it somewhat, the BOD, under the leadership of the new chairman, decides to call in an outside consultant to conduct a comprehensive analysis of the situation.

The consultant (appointed by the public sector) knows the McKinsey 7S framework well.

- He starts by making a quick initial analysis of the situation, mainly financial: revenue and changes in results over recent years, analysis of major expense items, gross operating mass, etc. Not only do his findings coincide with those of the administrative supervision, but they reinforce them by presenting significantly more severe results.

- Once this first 'official' observation is made, as the realisation of a mainly financial report does not specifically require presence on the ground, he works in the company and conducts workshops with the top managers. This shows a series of new findings, which highlight the deficiencies in organisation and logistics, internal tensions, competence issues, etc.
- Once the consultant clearly understands the missions and objectives of the company, his job is to make concrete recommendations. The solutions proposed are the result of the workshops, which are therefore in agreement or partnership with the company employees and will be partially implemented.
- Thus, X will be reorganised in depth: although the inevitable departure of a significant portion of the staff (a third of workers) by dismissal or early retirement is a lot to bear socially, it will not cause a strike.

By observing the consultant's approach, we realise that he begins his reflections starting from the core of the 7S framework. He first considers the values shared by workers in the execution of their work. He then focuses on the staff and their qualities and flaws. The problems are analysed in light of discrepancies between the system (such as procedures) and the staff. This shows, for example, that some missions are not clearly defined or are partially done twice, and many lack the tools or skills to perform the tasks assigned to them.

By clarifying the internal procedures, the consultant works on the system, but also on competencies at the same time.

He is also aware of a number of tensions, related to different personalities, but also to external political factors. As we have said, the number of workers increased sharply and quickly, with no changes to the service provided. Due to the politicisation of the BOD (a public company), some workers appear less 'legitimate' than others. In this particular situation, the consultant works with two newly arrived executives who are relatively unaffected by these issues of legitimacy: the financial manager and the Chairman of the BOD.

Despite the work dynamic and even, to some extent, because of it, tension and divisions are created between some workers, including the director of the company himself. The director feels a loss of legitimacy, with a number of his decisions and actions being questioned. Meanwhile, the Chairman is also involved: he acts as the interface between the workers and the BOD and provides important work that leads to a revitalisation of the entire BOD, with better information and greater involvement of members. These tensions reveal that, by working on the system, the consultant has shaken up the structure. The 'field' work has forced the structure to adapt to an inevitable and important reorganisation.

Led by the new managers, following the consultant's recommendations and with the support of most of the lower-level workers, the managers – the BOD – can redefine the company's strategy. Certainly, the missions are defined by an organic framework, but the way of acting on it is up to them. In this case, the strategy is as follows:

- adapting the method;
- setting targets in line with the company's mission and the values that underpin it. Since it is a public limited services company and did not position itself on the market in relation to private actors, the strategic aspect is more limited.

With regards to style, the change of Chairman is a determining factor: a certain dynamism and a new involvement now animate this management body. The director, put on the spot because of shortcomings that had been raised in various reports, and having not taken part in the consultant's work, is isolated. Abandoned by his board of directors, he chose to leave the company as part of an early retirement plan and the financial manager immediately replaced him. In a way, we come full circle since the financial manager and the president were the two main people who dealt with the consultant.

Remember that the reorganisation of company X was completed without social clashes (without strikes in particular). Today, the social climate is significantly better than it was in the past. It runs more harmoniously due to the redefinition of tasks and services. However, some details remain to be settled, including the fact that certain skills are still lacking internally. There are various reasons for this:

- Firstly, the current staff are generally underqualified.
- Secondly, from a regulatory point of view, because a company conducting a major restructuring cannot hire new staff over the next three years, it is necessary to determine how many employees are needed to continue the company's operations and level of service. This approach involves calculating the desired number of departures in order to form a small team, without necessarily having all the required skills.

Finally, we stress the fact that the consultant began his reflection from the centre of the 7S atom (shared values), i.e. from what all the workers have in common. Afterwards, he 'travelled' through the framework, which is perfectly acceptable. The components' interconnection and lack of hierarchy represent, in our opinion, one of the major strengths of the model.

SUMMARY

- The McKinsey 7S framework is an organisational diagnostic model used in management, particularly during the implementation of new projects or changes to be made within a company. Its success stems from the fact that it allows you to consider an interesting set of parameters, and emphasises their interconnection.
- Appearing in the 1980s, this model is the result of changes in social science (structuralism and enhancement of social relationships) and the economy (modification of commercial and business structures leading to hybridisation and internationalisation of companies).
- The theorists of the McKinsey 7S framework are Robert Waterman, Thomas Peters and Julien Philips.
- This model has the advantage of taking into account the interactions between the various aspects that make up an organisation. In addition, emphasis is placed on human relations and the qualitative aspect.
- However, this model, like all others, is still considered to be a tool and not an end in itself. Moreover, given the importance that it places on human relationships, shared values and management, it gives priority to subjective criteria or qualitative data. As such, some prefer approaches that are more focused on economic and quantifiable data.

We want to hear from you!
Leave a comment on your online library
and share your favourite books on social media!

FURTHER READING

BIBLIOGRAPHY

- Bajoit, G. (1992) *Pour une sociologie relationnelle*. Paris: PUF.
- Bourdieu, P. (1979) *La Distinction – critique sociale du jugement*. Paris: Éditions de Minuit.
- Bourdieu, P. (2002) *Questions de sociologie*. Paris: Éditions de Minuit.
- Crozier, M. and Friedberg, E. (1977) *L'Acteur et le Système*. Paris: Seuil.
- Desveaux, E. (2008) *Au-delà du structuralisme. Six méditations sur Claude Lévi-Strauss*. Paris: Complexe.
- Lévi-Strauss, C. (2003) *Anthropologie structurale*. Paris: Pocket.
- Tom Peters's website: http://tompeters.com/
- Waterman, R. H., Peters, T. J. and Philips, J. R. (1980) Structure is not Organization. *Business Horizons*. 23(3), pp. 14-26.

Made in the USA
Columbia, SC
01 October 2018